THE MODERN RULES OF *Style*

THE MODERN RULES OF *Style*

PAUL MARX

Defending Liberty
Pursuing Justice

Cover design by ABA Publishing.

09 08 07 06 05 5 4 3 2 1

Library of Congress Cataloging-in-Publication Data

Marx, Paul
The modern rules of style.
Paul Marx
Library of Congress Cataloging-in-Publication Data is on file.

ISBN 10: 1-59031-805-6
ISBN 13: 978-1-59031-805-8

Table of Contents

Foreword

Professor Marx has written a superb little book for lawyers. It's a thoughtful guide to sophisticated techniques for making your sentences work better. In fact, it might have been subtitled "Advanced Sentence-Writing for Lawyers."

Do we—the lawyers—really need help writing sentences? Yes, we do, because so much depends on our sentences: money, rights, property, and more. And so many people scrutinize our sentences: opposing counsel, clients, judges, and our bosses. With so much on the line and with so many audiences, we need to write better sentences than lawyers historically have. We need more training and more tools. This book will help.

But even though I can rightly describe the book as sophisticated and advanced, it is straightforward, too. The guidance Professor Marx gives is written in the kinds of sentences he advocates: planned and polished yet crisp and direct. He follows his own advice about parallelism, modifiers, and noun clauses. He recommends and then uses the colon, the semicolon, and the dash, and he uses them well. You can, too, because you will learn a great deal from the many examples. But you can and should imitate Professor Marx's writing style, too. All of us should.

Wayne Schiess
Director of Legal Writing
University of Texas School of Law

Introduction to Writing with Style

The purpose of this little book is to give you some suggestions for lifting your writing up from the humdrum and making it stand out. If you follow through on the tips given here, your writing will be more accurate, interesting, and distinctive. It will lead close readers of what you write to say to themselves: This is written by someone who really knows how to write. Using the types of sentences suggested here will separate your writing from that of most of your peers, whose writing will seem flat and routine.

Think of how you respond to the baseball pitcher who says, "I pitched *well* tonight." Most baseball players would not say *well*; they would say *good*. When you hear a ball player say *well*, you think he is a cut above. In writing, word choices count for even more than they do in conversation. But once you have achieved a reasonable command of diction, the kinds of sentences you put together determine the impression your writing makes. The combination of diction and types of sentences defines your writing style.

This book is not for people who have problems with basic diction or grammar. It is intended for professionals who write well enough to get by but who would like to give their writing some distinction and have it stand out. Lawyers write every day, but often they do not have a sense of style. They are unaware of the variety of sentences available to them. They get what they have to say down on paper—but without distinction.

At the time of his confirmation hearings, one of Chief Justice John G. Roberts's former colleagues at the firm of Hogan & Hartson spoke about Judge Roberts's concern for good writing. David G. Leitch, who went on to be the general counsel to the Ford Motor Company, was reported by *The New York Times*, as having said about Roberts that it was his view that the writing of a lawyer "conveys not only your argument to the court, but it also conveys a sense of your credibility and the care with which you put together your case."

At the end of his first term as chief justice, Roberts's writing style again was praised. Professor Akhil Amar of Yale Law School referred to two sentences from Roberts's opinions that conveyed the economy and elegance of his writing. In *Gonzalez v. O Centro Espirita*, Roberts wrote: "The government's argument echoes the classic rejoinder of bureaucrats throughout history: If I make an exception for you, I'll have to make one for everybody, so no exceptions." A considerable part of the success of that sentence is due to Chief Justice Roberts's use of the colon. One of the chapters in this book is devoted to such effective uses of the colon. The second sentence to which Professor Amar referred is from *Jones v. Flowers*. Here is what Roberts wrote: "In response to the returned form suggesting that Jones had not received notice that he was about to lose his property, the state did—nothing." Professor Amar commented, "That little dash is brilliant." It helps "every ordinary citizen understand the frustration of dealing with government stupidity." The effective use of the dash is the subject of another chapter in this book.

Following the suggestions in the chapters ahead will definitely increase your credibility and the economy and elegance of your style. You will begin to put together types of sentences that you rarely wrote before. While your letters, briefs, memos, or reports may have gotten your message across and have been free of errors, there might have been little to suggest that you thought much about the best way to say what needed to be said. The opportunity that writing offers to enhance credibility will have been lost.

The New Yorker magazine sportswriter Roger Angell is the stepson of the great *New Yorker* essayist E. B. White. Angell remembers vividly those days in his childhood when White worked on his weekly *New Yorker* essay. The sounds of White's typewriter could be heard only in spurts; in between were long silences. Young Roger wondered what was going on. Well, what was going on was that White was editing and revising—adding, deleting, changing—mulling things over in his head before going ahead and hitting the keys some more. White usually knew what he wanted to write about. But he wanted his writing to express his own style. If he did not care whether what he wrote was distinctive, he could have gotten his relatively brief columns done in a fraction of the time he spent on them. One of the main qualities of White's style is its tone of casualness. But his sentences did not always come out of his head in a way that sounded casual. He had to tinker with his sentences to gain that tone. If White had turned in his first drafts, he never would have attained his reputation as a great essayist.

What White worked on were not matters of correctness; grammar and other basics were second nature. What he did, first of all, was to make sure he would not be misunderstood. He sought words that were accurate and vivid. Because he wanted his sentences to convey attitude as well as information, he tried to avoid sentences that were flat. He wanted to make the voice of E. B. White distinctive; not fancy, just distinctive. That took work. Good writing doesn't come out ready for market on a first draft. In making his changes, White made use of a range of sentence patterns that might not occur to everyone who writes. When you are preoccupied with your content, when your main concern is getting the idea or information down, it's hard to deal with matters of style or fine points of meaning.

Awareness of these sentence patterns and their use will help you come closer to what you really want to say and to emphasize. The more sentence patterns you know, the better chance you have of finding a way to convey subtlety and nuance. While the sentence patterns presented in this book certainly are not the only ones that could be presented, the use of these patterns are most likely to improve the overall quality of your writing and to make bland writing distinctive.

The Method

Each chapter begins with a general explanation of a particular type of sentence. The examples of that kind of sentence proceed from the simple to the longer and more complex. That progression, by the way, does not imply that the longer, more complex sentence is the better, stronger sentence. As a general rule, the shorter the sentence the stronger it is. The shorter a sentence is the more emphasis its idea will get. There is artistry in the making of both short and long. Inevitably, a powerful brief sentence is the result of a sorting out of ideas and a careful paring down; a clearly structured and more detailed longer sentence is the result of a careful aligning of clauses and a mastery of the conventions of punctuation. In most strong paragraphs, there is a role for both the longer and the shorter (More on this in Chapter 10).

Many of the illustrative sentences demonstrate not only the pattern under discussion but also other techniques discussed in the book. In the final chapter, Chapter 12, you will see five passages of excellent writing that make use of different combinations of the ten patterns discussed earlier. As you become more sensitive to these different types of sentences, your desire to use them will be reinforced as you begin to notice their presence in good writing.

Some writers will use one or more of these patterns rather heavily, and not use others at all. If a writer is a frequent user of parallelism (Chapter 2), the semi-colon (Chapter 6), and the dash (Chapter 8), that then will be a characteristic of that writer's style. Another writer might like to use noun clauses (Chapter 5) and trailing modifiers (Chapter 4). Still another might go heavy with the colon (Chapter 7). Someone else will find appeal in using the power of comparisons (Chapter 9) and short, pointed statements (Chapter 10). There is no rule that says a required portion of sentences must use one technique or another. Which techniques a writer uses is a matter of the complexity of the material but also of things like the writer's depth of conviction, his flair for the dramatic, his confidence.

Knowing the difference between a dependent clause and an independent clause is essential to being able to construct types of sentences that are acceptable to experienced readers. The discussion at the top of Chapter 3 will be helpful in this regard. If you should not feel certain of your ability to use the various patterns as you go through the book, you'll find it helpful to study the differences between the first drafts and possible revisions in each chapter and also to carry out the suggestions for practice. In any case, take your time and try not to digest too much too quickly.

Three Ducks in a Row:

Use Parallelism

Whenever the opportunity presents itself, a good writer will use parallelism. Parallelism is a way of showing the more or less equal importance and close relationship of things, ideas, or qualities. That is done by the repetition of the same grammatical form, whether it be adjectives or adverbs, nouns, verbs, or combinations of words. The most common form of parallelism is the series of three. Linking three of a kind usually makes a sentence stronger. Linking two of a kind is also desirable, but if three, or more, of a kind can be linked the sentence will be more persuasive and more rhythmic. Readers are pleased when they begin to hear a rhythm as they read; that's why poets and songwriters make frequent use of parallelism. The writer who creates a rhythm will give the reader another reason to respond favorably. But tact must be used; overdo it, and you will lose the reader's respect.

Adjectives

The courtroom was *windowless*, *cluttered*, and *dirty*.

The prosecutor was *uninformed*, *arrogant*, and *histrionic*.

The judge's face was memorable—*earthy*, *authoritative*, and *mean*.

The decision was *ambiguous*, *equivocal* and, worst of all, *unenforceable*.

Nouns

The main costs of airlines are *salaries*, *fuel*, and *insurance*.

Supported by *engineers*, *doctors*, and *cyclists*, the attorney for the plaintiff made a strong case that the bicycle was defective.

Blueprints, *maps*, *photographs*, and *videos* were all used to demonstrate that the zoning change was a mistake.

With *towns*, *townships*, *boroughs*, *counties*, and *states*, American local government can be very confusing.

In the first two sentences, we have two series of three nouns. In the third and fourth sentences, we have longer series. Another reason to go for at least three of a kind is that citing three instances makes a point more believable than one or two would.

As in the sentence below, nouns in a series often have modifiers in front of them or following them.

The troubled *neighborhood* had some beautiful *homes*,

streets with boarded-up *windows*, and *corners* that were open-air drug markets.

The noun homes *is modified by the single-word adjective in front of it.* Streets *is followed by a prepositional phrase that functions as an adjective.* Corners *is followed by a relative clause that functions as an adjective.*

Verbs

Like nouns, verbs in a series can be modified. In the second and third sentences below, the verbs are modified by adverbs—and one adverbial phrase. In the fourth sentence, three of the verbs are modified by adverbial phrases.

He *blocked*, *tackled*, and *cheered*.

He *ran* adequately, *passed* poorly, and *blocked* cowardly.

The board members *discussed* the issue interminably, reluctantly *voted*, and *adjourned* with relief.

At most board meetings, members of the audience *fidget* restlessly, *converse* with their neighbors, *get annoyed* at something, and *leave* before the end.

It is unusual for a writer to construct sentences with grammatically correct parallelism in a first draft. In the course of revising a first draft, a writer often will see opportunities to bring together several things or qualities that are closely related, and work them into a series with the same grammatical form. Economy in writing is very desirable, and effective parallelism tightens sentences and paragraphs.

Phrases, Predicates, Clauses

Combinations of words in phrases and clauses also can be put into parallel form.

Near the gate, *inside the portal*, and *at our seats*, we were asked to show our identification cards.

Here we have three prepositional phrases—beginning with the prepositions near, inside, *and* at—*that convey the order and the locations of the requests to show identification. If you were giving an account of attending a football game, so many other things could have been in your mind as you were writing, that in your first draft you miss the opportunity to link those identification requests in parallel phrases.*

Today's airline pilots *make less money than they used to*, *are away from home for longer stretches*, and *worry about their eventual retirement pay*.

Here we have three parallel predicates. The subject for all three is the word pilots. *In one sentence the writer notes three issues in the lives of airline pilots.*

In driving a car, there are some situations that require a particularly high level of alertness: *when you back up*, *when you* come *to* a *stop sign*, and *when you make* a *left turn*.

Here the three groups of words beginning with when *are clauses, because they each have a subject and verb. To be more specific, they are dependent clauses, and cannot stand alone as sentences. They also are* adverb clauses *because each clause tells* when *about the verb* require. *If you were writing about your experience learning how to drive, you might have been focusing on where you drove and not have realized as you were getting down all that information that some situations behind the wheel require more alertness. You realize that you can be more interesting if you go into the when as well as the where. You realize that an effective way to set up a discussion of those situations is, first of all, to bring them together with parallelism.*

The New York Times recently thought about finding a better way of handling its corrections. Editors realized that not all corrections are equally important, and decided to make a change. It wasn't easy to write the four brief paragraphs in which the change in policy was conveyed to the paper's readers. But the writer realized that there were three basic types of corrections: minor errors, errors that caused confusion, and errors that were caused by bad judgment. "For the Record" would deal with minor errors like the spelling of a name, "Corrections" would deal with confusion caused by unclear writing, and an "Editor's Note" would deal with statements that showed bad judgment by the writer. The hard part in writing the four paragraphs stating the new policy was explaining what constituted bad judgment. Experienced journalists probably would have little difficulty in spotting instances of bad judgment. But how do you refer to the various kinds of instances? Well, the writer resorted to parallelism and summed them up as instances that lacked *fairness*, *balance*, or *perspective*. The writer undoubtedly had to make a lot of changes before discovering that what he wanted to say could be conveyed with those three parallel nouns.

Can you spot the other uses of parallelism in the above paragraph? Have you noted that independent clauses as well as dependent clauses can be stated in parallel form within a single sentence?

Relatively inexperienced writers often have a prejudice against repetition. They want to avoid repeating a word or group of words. Such writers sometimes will pick up a thesaurus and hunt for substitute words they can plug in and thereby avoid the supposed sin of repetition. And this prejudice leads to the notion that repeating a grammatical form is also undesirable. Reinforcing that notion is the principle that says variation of sentence structure is a mark of good writing. Varied sentence structure *is* a mark of good writing—but so is the skillful use of repetition.

As you seek opportunities to use parallelism, you might find yourself excluding certain information, certain details. You must remember that parallelism is not an end in itself. If you think the details help your writing more than the parallelism would, then keep the details, tighten up as best you can, and let the opportunity for parallelism pass. Different writers have different values and, therefore, different styles. Some value succinctness more, some value the vividness of details, and some manage to be succinct and vivid.

Outstanding Examples

Here's a sentence from Margaret Mitchell's *Gone with the Wind* about the types of men who made up a company of Confederate soldiers from Georgia: "Rich planters were few in the young county of Clayton, and, in order to muster a full-strength troop, it had been necessary to raise more recruits among the *sons* of small farmers, *hunters* in the backwoods, swamp *trappers*, *Crackers*, and, in a very few cases, even poor *whites*, if they were above the average of their class."

A recent book about 18th Century Scottish intellectuals, *Crowded with Genius* by James Buchan, says some interesting things about Edinburgh and its people. Here, paraphrased, is a passage illustrating Buchan's use of parallelism: The city had its *towers*, its ancient *castle*, and a superb wide *street* running down its center. The diet of most of the people consisted of *fish*, *pottage*, *milk*, bitter *kale*, and a great *deal* of home-brewed small beer. Everyone—and that includes children—drank *whisky*, *claret*, *rum*, and *ale*.

First Draft

What follows is a loosely written paragraph that could benefit from some tightening up with parallelism.

John Daggett grew up in the mold of an old-time good 'ole boy. The summer before ninth grade he moved to a small town in Georgia. A year later, his father found work on shrimp boat in Louisiana. He got tired of that pretty quickly and moved the family to western Texas, where he became a wildcatter in the oil fields. John started to drink at fourteen, when he looked old enough to get away with sitting at bar stools and chugging beer. Bars were a good location for picking up girls, and he did that with alarming frequency. He learned to tinker with cars, and engaged in weekly drag-racing, even though the local police were always cracking down. Despite all the diversions, he managed to graduate from high school and enroll at Texas A&M. He did not like college. Chemistry and sociology were particularly boring. But he was not a good student. He flunked out after two semesters. So he joined the army as a buck private. He liked the army and advanced quickly. He became an officer. In 1968, he was sent to Vietnam.

Possible Revision

John Daggett grew up in the mold of an old-time good 'ole boy. As an adolescent he lived in Georgia, Louisiana, and Texas. At an early age, he drank in bars, picked up older girls, and broke the law by drag-racing. But he graduated from high school and enrolled at Texas A&M. He flunked out, joined the army, became an officer, and was sent to Vietnam.

Practice

For practice in using parallelism, revise the following paragraph and go for as much parallelism as you think the passage can stand.

John Daggett came of age in Vietnam. He was in combat against the guerrillas for a year. When he came home he wrote about it in a notebook he gave to his grandfather, who was an army captain in World War II. In the field, he said, he could never tell when bullets might come zinging out of the jungle. He was always afraid that he or one of his men would step on a mine and be blown to bits. At night, when he tried to sleep, he listened for that first mortar round flying toward you. When he was back at camp, it was still dangerous. There too you never knew when you would come under attack from mortars. The environment there was not pleasant at all despite the beautiful landscape. It was almost always hot. When it rained, it didn't stop. There was always dust in the air from the trucks. When you blew your nose, the handkerchief turned brown. The constant smell of diesel exhaust was sickening. And then there were the leeches going after your blood. He said he would rather look out for snakes than deal with leeches. He said he would rather have dry clothes and a real meal every day than have a local girl friend.

Starting Out:
Use Introductory Modifiers

Placing a modifier in front of a sentence's *independent clause* (sometimes called the *main clause*) and setting it off with a comma will give the modifier emphasis and vary the construction of your sentences. Also, such a sentence usually will change the rhythm in the flow of sentences, and make the whole paragraph more interesting.

In order to be called a clause, a group of words must have a verb and a subject of the verb. An *independent* clause is a clause that can stand alone and be a sentence. If, however, it has a certain kind of word at the beginning, the clause will be a *dependent* clause, and if it stands alone will *not* be a sentence. Such words as *if*, *when*, *while*, *whereas*, *although*, and *because*, called subordinating conjunctions, subordinate—or reduce—a clause and make it into a *dependent clause*.

Another kind of dependent clause follows a noun, and, acting like an adjective, tells something more about the noun. This kind of dependent clause has a first word that is called a *relative pronoun*; it connects the modifying clause to the noun it modifies. The most frequently used relative pronouns are *who*, *whose*, *which*, and *that*. Being able to tell a dependent clause from an independent clause is a necessity for good writing.

When experienced readers note that a sentence does not begin with an independent clause, they shift gears in order to receive the modifier(s) that precede the independent clause. Also, they expect that the subject of the independent clause will be modified by the introductory modifier; sometimes, even good writers mess this up. If the sentence is structured as expected, the reader will feel a bond with the writer, and the writer will gain credibility with the reader. The reader will think the writer knows how to craft a good sentence. Here are some examples of effective introductory modifiers.

Single-Word Adjectives

Weary, he fell asleep as the plane landed.

Frustrated again, he left the meeting in despair.

Tall, *dark*, and *handsome*, the defense attorney silenced the room when he entered.

Prepositional Phrases

Before the recess, the proceeding was chaotic.

During the break, the defense attorney conferred with the prosecutor.

With much tact, he made his opponent see the weakness in his case.

Between the two of them, there had been years of animosity.

After two more hours of back and forth, he talked to his client, who nodded with satisfaction.

Unlike the partners at the firm, who set their own hours, the associates had to be in by nine and could not leave before five.

Verbal Adjectives

A *verbal* is a form of a verb, usually with the ending *ed* or *ing*, that can be used as an adjective. Verbals can be very useful in conveying an emotional state. They get more emphasis by being placed at the beginning of a sentence.

Excited, she slipped and fell.

Elated, the winner leaped over the net.

Stopped, the trucker said all the wrong things to the police officer.

Confused, he called his mother instead of his wife.

Depressed, he began to look for another job.

Fuming, he punched the wall and fractured his wrist.

Cycling, he returned home much later than usual.

Arguing, he felt a rush of adrenaline.

Verbal Phrases

A *verbal phrase* is a form of a verb followed by a related group of words. A *verbal phrase* can be very effective as an adjective at the beginning of a sentence.

Sawing the board, he continued to watch the bird.

Conferring with his partners, he began to shift his position.

Thinking he had been treated like dirt, the associate decided to look for another job.

Wanting to avoid ambiguities, he struggled with the introductory section of the trust agreement.

Changing legalese into plain English, he smiled with satisfaction.

Cutting and pasting several sections the next morning, he put the document into its final form.

Sitting across from a person talking on a cell, he gave up trying to read.

Paying twenty-five dollars for the taxi ride, he got home before dark.

Working out after a long day of work, she tripped and fell off the treadmill.

An Outstanding Example

"Doggedly *navigating* with stick or crutch, slouch-*hatted*, fabulously *bearded*, *drinking like a comradely fish*, Henley became a landmark in literary London—critic, editor, poet, spottily learned, quarrelsome as a musketeer, fond as a woman of ill-natured gossip, talking like a fire-hose, detested here, greatly loved there—particularly by young men whom he helped to launch such as Wells, Kipling, and Yeats." (J. C. Furnas in *Voyage to Windward: The Life of Robert Louis Stevenson.)*

First Draft

The Iraq War was the major issue in the presidential election. President Bush accused Senator Kerry of flip-flopping. He said Kerry voted for going to war and then criticized him for doing just that—going to war. Kerry said he voted to give the president the authority to go to war. But he said he did not give the president his approval to go to war. Some voters felt they were caught in the middle, They did not like what either candidate was saying, so they decided to vote for Ralph Nader.

Possible Revision

The Iraq War was the major issue in the presidential election. *Disdaining* inconsistency, President Bush accused Senator Kerry of flip-flopping. *Repeating* again and again that Kerry criticized him for going to war but that he himself had voted to go to war, the president hoped to demonstrate Kerry's inconsistency. Kerry answered the charge. *Voting* to give the president the authority to go war, *he* did not intend to give the president his approval to start the war. Some voters felt they were caught in the middle. *Unwilling* to cast their vote for either President Bush or Senator Kerry, they voted for Ralph Nader.

Practice

Revise the following paragraph so that two sentences have introductory modifiers.

The governor wanted to take the profit out of the drug trade. He realized that boys in the neighborhoods saw the drug dealers as their role models. The boys dressed like the dealers. They talked like them. And, worst of all, they started carrying guns. The governor thought something had to be done. He proposed a law that provided for the state to open shops that would sell marijuana, cocaine, and heroin. When customers came in to make their purchases, they would be given information about getting treatment for their addictions. He hoped that such stores would put the street-corner dealers out of business.

Closing Strong:
Use Trailing Modifiers

The trailing modifier—the modifier that follows a sentence's independent clause and is separated from it with a comma—gives the reader a sense of fullness. Something has been said that can stand alone as a sentence. But then the comma slows things down, allowing the reader to take a breath and easily digest another piece of information. When that happens, the reader feels grateful, for the change of pace and for the additional things learned.

One of the most common frameworks for a trailing modifier, which, coming after the independent clause, is not necessary for the grammatical integrity and meaning of the sentence, is the dependent clause that begins with a relative pronoun. When the relative pronoun is *who*, *whose*, *which*, or *that*, the clause functions as an adjective and says something more about the noun immediately in front of it.

When the pronoun is *where* or *when*, the clause functions as an adverb. Sometimes it says something more about the time or place immediately before it. Sometimes it says something more about the whole preceding independent clause. When trailing modifiers are in the form of a *participial phrase*—a phrase beginning with an *ing* word or an *ed* word—they not only can give an explanation or additional information but can indicate a *causal* relationship. Sentences with trailing modifiers will be longer, but that is no reason to avoid writing them. So long as they are connected and punctuated in ways that are expected, readers will appreciate them.

A common error is the failure to use a comma after the independent clause. If the independent clause is by itself definitive—could stand alone without additional information—then use the comma. Do not use a comma when the additional information is essential to what you want to say.

Who, Whose, Which

She was very upset about the illness of her boss, *who* was the only boss she ever admired.

In 2004, some voters disliked both George W. Bush and John Kerry, *who* had had privileged childhoods and seemed out of touch with the common man.

To the surprise of few in New York, the Democratic candidate for the U. S. Senate in 2000 was Hillary Clinton, *who* had been longing to get into public life as her own person.

When the person spoken of is not clearly identified, do not use a comma before who.

They disliked the secretary *who* was always making personal calls.

All the members of the board were men *who* had worked their way to the top.

The board meeting would be a referendum on the chairman, *whose* personality irritated just about everybody.

The senior partner thought it was very important to learn as much as possible about your adversary, *whose* habits and lifestyle could be used against him.

In a way, the work of a new associate is like basic training, *which* is designed to turn a soft civilian into a hardened warrior.

The School of Law encouraged its students to be aware of the human dimensions of their writing, *which* could make vivid what the lives of their clients were like.

They always had a big debate about Columbus Day, *which*, the owner said, should not be considered a real holiday.

She was not happy about working in a fifty-story building, *which* in case of fire would lose its elevators and *whose* stairwells were extremely narrow.

Avoid using which *and* that *interchangeably.* Which, *followed by a comma, is used when the preceding noun is definitive.* That, *not followed by a comma, is used when the preceding noun is not definitive.*

The grandparents moved to Bethesda, *which* is just across the line from Washington, D. C.

The couple bought a McMansion *that* was way out in the exurbs.

It is the only airline *that* still serves complete meals.

To Tell Where or When

General Tommy Franks briefly attended the University of Texas, *where* he joined a fraternity and drank heavily.

Mr. Walker was a long-time member and former deacon and head of the stewardship committee at the Downtown Baptist Church, *where* a memorial service will be held at 1 p.m. Wednesday.

The philosopher David Hume neither married nor had a mistress, though he enjoyed female company in both Edinburgh and Paris, *where* he was well known as a ladies' man.

The humor of the situation struck him, and he laughed and looked up at the clear sky, *where* all the stars seemed to be winking over his embarrassment.

The school began to teach parents of its pupils in the 1960s, *when* adult illiteracy came to the nation's attention.

The worst year of the Vietnam War was 1968, *when* the Tet offensive turned American opinion against the war.

There is hope that there will be no more war after every war, *when* people have had enough of killing and believe everyone feels the same way.

He felt great anxiety during the months of Standard Time, *when* he always tried to get home before total darkness fell.

To State a Causal Relationship

A trailing modifier in the form of a participial phrase is an effective way of quickly indicating cause and effect or effect and cause.

It became apparent there were not enough troops in

Baghdad to uphold law and order [Cause], *causing* the exhilaration of being there to quickly disappear [Effect].

Soon after the bombing, Israel was quick to blame al-Qaeda [Effect], *noting* the sophistication and scale of the attacks [Cause].

Voltaire's knowledge of science was surprisingly deep [Cause], *demonstrating* the accessibility of Newton's ideas to the layman [Effect].

The microscopic resistors in printer cartridges heat rapidly [Cause], *propelling* the ink out of the nozzles [Effect].

To Give an Explanation

It seemed like an impossible choice, *putting* two strongly held values into direct conflict.

A writer is like a hunter, sometimes *waiting* in the blind for something to suddenly turn up, sometimes *roaming* through the woods in hopes of finding something unexpected.

Professional football has become America's most popular form of entertainment, *uniting* people of all classes, races, and backgrounds but also *dividing* them because of their strong allegiance to their favorite teams.

To Give Additional Information

The professor stayed out of the Vietnam War, *deferred* by being a graduate student.

She was unsuccessful in getting into the writing seminar, *rejected* again and *separated* from her friends.

General Franks grew up in Oklahoma and Texas, did tours of duty in Vietnam and other hot spots, and ended up as commander of CENTCOM in Tampa, *spending* whole days in bunker-like rooms filled with plasma screens and lots of acronyms.

Outstanding Examples

"Four score and seven years ago our fathers brought forth upon this continent a new nation, *conceived* in liberty and *dedicated* to the proposition that all men are created equal." (Abraham Lincoln)

Clearly distracted, he broke off the conversation, rose from the table, and walked slowly toward the lobby, *looking* in all directions, *scrutinizing* everyone, *tracking* the source of every unusual noise.

Isaiah Thomas said that when he was at Indiana and listened to Coach Bob Knight it was as if he were hearing his mother on tape, *talking* about doing the right thing, *living* the right way, *going* to class, *working* hard, and *being* a gentleman.

In 2003, about 12 million of the 18 million overseas visitors to the United States came from the twenty-seven nations, most of them European, that will now be required to participate in the fingerprinting program, according to the Travel Industry Association of America, *which* represents the nation's largest airlines, hotels, cruise lines, and car-rental companies.

First Draft

The newspaper industry is not doing well. Poor earnings this year is another sign of uneven performance in the industry. It is an industry full of paradoxes. A shrug of the shoulders was the only answer given by one CEO. The earnings of his eighteen papers were thoroughly mixed. Papers in the largest markets did not perform as well as papers in smaller and midsize markets. That makes no sense. Classified-ad revenue varies mysteriously. It doesn't always go down when jobs are scarce. Real estate and automotive advertising differ from classified. That's especially true in the populous East. There people tend to be more cautious.

Possible Revision

The newspaper industry is not doing too well. Poor earnings this year is another sign of uneven performance in the industry, *which* is full of paradoxes. A shrug of the shoulders was the only answer given by one CEO, *whose* company owns eighteen papers. Papers in the largest markets did not perform as well as papers in smaller and midsize markets, *which* makes no sense. Advertising revenue is inexplicably volatile. That is especially true of classified ads. Revenue should be down in a soft economy, *when* fewer jobs would be advertised. But it's not. It is down, however, in automotive and real estate, especially in the populous East, *where* people tend to be more cautious.

Practice

With a trailing modifier after a comma, add information or give an explanation to each independent clause that follows. Make use of *where, when, who, whose, which.*

She changed planes at O'Hare

She said she could be reached at the Marriott

Keeping a straight face, he announced that the next sales managers' meeting would take place in Hawaii

One of the biggest shopping periods of the year is late August

An important unofficial American holiday is Super Bowl Sunday

One of the most memorable dates in American history is December 7, 1941

He said he would have no objection at all if the company fired our sales manager

A person of growing importance in the health industry is the nurse practitioner

It is doubtful that there ever was a more important businessman than Bill Gates

When the last study was completed, Merck acted quickly to shut down sales of Vioxx

Apple Computer announced that its fourth quarter sales were unexpectedly high due to the popularity of its iPod music players

A major controversy in the American corporate world is whether to deduct from profits the value of stock options

A case in point was the shortage of flu vaccine

The maestro offended the adults but was cheered by the students

What's What:
Use the Noun Clause

The Noun Clause is a dependent clause that is used in the same way single-word nouns are used. Noun Clauses, then, can be used as subjects of sentences, as predicate nouns, as direct objects of verbs, or as objects of prepositions. Noun Clauses usually have *what*, *that*, *why*, or *how* as their first word. These are the relative pronouns that are most commonly used, but other words can serve the same function.

Relatively inexperienced writers rarely use the Noun Clause. When experienced readers see a Noun Clause, they know they are in the hands of a skillful writer. To increase your credibility, try to use an occasional Noun Clause.

As the Subject of a Sentence

What turns him off is phoniness.

What makes him most happy is a walk in the woods by himself.

What made his work so important was the effect it had on other investors.

What the rank-and-file union members wanted was the resignation of the union's president.

What is intriguing is *that this day might be the turning point.*

What is heartening is the large turn-out; *what is disheartening* is *that they did not understand.*

That the president is the commander-in-chief is stated in the Constitution.

That he worked day and night for the cause cannot be disputed.

That Supreme Court nominees refuse to answer certain kinds of questions is a new development.

As a Predicate Noun

That is *what the president did.*

That is *why the president did it.*

That is *what the quarterback thought he should do.*

What you see is *what you get.*

What I heard from some of my classmates at the reunion was *that those who didn't come were people who had reached a plateau in their careers.*

As the Direct Object of a Verb

The policeman asked *what had happened.*

The career of the senior partner demonstrated *how hard it was to rise in this firm.*

Many Republicans believed *that Kerry was a hypocrite.*

From the outset, the president's aides said *that the election would be a referendum on the president's leadership.*

Many who strongly support the war on terrorism argue *that "war on terror" is a flawed concept.*

Voters who were undecided frequently asserted *that they believed both candidates said what they thought people wanted to hear rather than what they really believed.*

As the Object of a Preposition

The defense attorney said we should give the defendant credit for *what he says he believes.*

But when you listen carefully to *what was said*, you have your doubts.

The trial turned ugly after *what both sides acknowledged were attempts to settle.*

When pressed on Iraq, both candidates talked about *what the catastrophe of 9/11 meant* and *how tough decisions had to be made.*

That boundaries between nations had become more porous is one of the things he meant by *what he called "the dark side of globalization."*

Outstanding Examples

What everyone said who watched the debates is *that* they got a good sense of who George W. Bush and John Kerry are, *what* they believe, and *how* they would approach the task of running the country.

"They noticed for the first time *how* her green eyes danced, *how* deep her dimples were when she laughed, *how* tiny her hands and feet were and *what* a small waist she had." (About Scarlett O'Hara in *Gone with the Wind.*)

First Draft

The story about the reservists in Iraq was unusual. When they refused a direct order, the reservists took a very drastic step. They had been asked to transport supplies over a dangerous route, and they said they wouldn't do it, because their vehicles were not adequately equipped. Relatives at home supported them. To them, these soldiers were brave; for they could face severe punishment. The soldiers thought they might have a problem when they first reported for duty and found badly maintained vehicles. Relatives remembered this, and backed them up. The Army says the equipment was not as bad as the soldiers say.

Possible Revision

The story about the reservists in Iraq was not *what you would expect to hear about a unit in the U.S. Army.* Members of a quartermaster company took *what has to be considered a very drastic step.* They refused a direct order. When asked to transport supplies over a dangerous route, they said *that their vehicles were not adequately equipped.* Relatives at home said *what had happened to them reflects problems in other units.* They said *what these soldiers did required great courage,* for they could be subject to severe punishment. Parents and wives asserted *that when the soldiers reported to their units in their home states they were disturbed by the condition of the equipment accompanying them to Iraq.* Greatly upset, relatives *said that the condition of the equipment became an issue because the soldiers needed well-maintained vehicles on what would be very danger-*

ous missions. What the facts are is in dispute. One thing is indisputable: the Army cannot give its soldiers the option to refuse an order.

Practice

Mark the Noun Clauses in the following paragraph.

He argued that a liberal arts education is invaluable. For what it does is teach human values, the value of logic, and the importance of inquiry and discovery. That he saw the intersection of the humanities and medicine changed what he had planned for his career. He decided to attend a research university instead of a stand-alone liberal arts college. What he wanted was an opportunity to participate in research during his four years as an undergraduate.

Looking Backward:
Use the Semi-Colon

Chapter Six

Occasional use of the semi-colon can have a dramatic effect. Like a period, the semi-colon brings the reader to a full stop. Unlike the period, the semi-colon signals that more will be said about what just has been said, whereas the period tells the reader that what follows will be a step forward. Mediocre writers try to avoid getting tangled up with semi-colons; however, when the semi-colon is used, and used correctly, the experienced reader will be impressed. Such sentences will stand out.

The semi-colon is used correctly when there is an independent clause before it, and another independent clause following it. That's what most inexperienced writers don't know; they use the semi-colon without taking note of the kind of clauses involved. The semi-colon can be used in a few other situations, but 95 percent of the time, it is used with two independent clauses. Never, never use the semi-colon following the salutation in a letter.

Use the Semi-Colon to Set Up a Contrast

The most effective use of the semi-colon is for the clash of opposites. The briefer the independent clauses, the more powerful the sentence.

She danced; he sat.
She won; he lost.
He said yes; she said no.
We are loyal; they are traitors.
Their strength is their offense; our strength is defense.

Scientists work in obscurity; ballplayers' deeds are in box scores every morning.

What she was prepared for was the likelihood of rejection; what she was not prepared for was indifference.

He was thoroughly disgusted by ugliness; beauty made him forgive the worst of incivilities.

Use the Semi-Colon to Elaborate or Explain

Use the first independent clause to make a general statement; use the second independent clause to elaborate or explain.

Nobel Prizes are awards for past performance; they are often given decades after the achievement.

Inducement prizes are different; a payout is necessary only if the stated goal is achieved.

Hume believed the laws of nature could be proved by repeated experiments; he believed the acceptance of miracles denied man's ability to separate what is true from what is false.

It is hard to pin down what Abraham Lincoln believed God's role is; he occasionally spoke about God but never relied upon God.

Al-Zarqawi set out for Afghanistan in 1989 and arrived too late; the Soviet Union had already withdrawn its troops.

One of his biggest mistakes was in his role as commander-in-chief; he flew out to an aircraft carrier and proclaimed that the mission had been accomplished.

Sometimes a Modifier Helps

The second independent clause frequently begins with an adverb—a conjunctive adverb, to be precise. The most commonly used conjunctive adverbs are the following: however, *which signals a contrast or a condition contrary to what was expected;* therefore, *which signals an effect, a result, or consequence;* furthermore, *which signals something in addition; and* indeed, *which is used for emphasis. In most cases, a comma should follow the conjunctive adverb.*

They lost the game; *however*, they were not unhappy with the way they played.

The mayor of Washington, D.C., had served time in jail; *however*, that did not stop his followers from nominating him again.

He was stopped for speeding, brought to the police station, and locked in a cell overnight; *therefore*, he was unable to attend the testimonial dinner in his honor.

The coach failed to win half his games; *therefore*, he got ready to move and to look for a new job.

He was charged a hefty fine; *furthermore*, his lawyer charged him a hefty fee.

The judge was told that Mr. Simmons had been divorced twice before and owed thousands in child support; *furthermore*, his favorite vacation spot was Las Vegas.

The Scottish philosophers were not like the French; *indeed*, they were unlike any other group of philosophers.

The philosophy professors always rooted for the underdog; *indeed*, they even rooted against the college's own teams.

Sometimes the second independent clause is preceded by a prepositional phrase that functions the same way as the conjunctive adverb.

The public works department assumed the parade would take place; *on the other hand*, the police went about their usual daily routines.

She loved shopping on holidays; *for example*, Presidents' Day was one of the most exciting days of the year for her.

He loved watching the NFL on TV on Sundays; *in addition*, he hardly ever missed a Friday night high school game.

She loved romantic comedies; *in fact*, she had seen every one of Hugh Grant's movies.

The highlight of their New Year's Eve was the dropping of the ball in Times Square; *despite her fear of being cold*, she went along.

Either of the two independent clauses can have a modifying dependent clause in front of it or after it.

When he was stopped for speeding and brought to the police station, he asked to make a phone call; he called his hometown lawyer.

He was stopped for speeding and brought to the police station; *when he was asked whether he'd like to make a phone call*, he said he would.

Although they usually did not bet, this time they did; they bet on all the underdogs.

Usually they did not bet; yesterday, they bet on all the underdogs, *although they knew that was foolish.*

An Outstanding Example

It is important to know the difference between being loyal, which is a good thing, and being obedient, which can be positively evil; loyalty is given voluntarily to higher-ups who deserve it, but obedience is given involuntarily to bosses who demand it.

First Draft

No country on earth has as much diversity as India. It has numerous religions, including Hinduism, Islam, and Christianity. It has numerous castes, of which the Brahmins are at the top, and numerous ethnic groups, such as Aryan, Dravidian, and Mongoloid. It also has sixteen languages. Between the 17th and 19th centuries, the British colonized India, taking control of government, the bureaucracy, and industry and assuming a social position above all Indians.

Possible Revision

No country on earth has as much diversity as India. It has numerous religions and ethnic groups. Among the religions are Hinduism, Islam, and Christianity; among the ethnic groups are Aryans, Dravidians, and Mongoloids. It also has sixteen languages and numerous castes, of which the Brahmins are at the top. Between the 17th and 19th centuries, the British colonized India; they took control of almost all the country's institutions and assumed a social position above all Indians.

Practice

In a daily newspaper, find three sentences using the semicolon. Write three sentences of your own that have the same structures as those in the newspaper.

Double Dot Means a Lot:

Use the Colon

Chapter Seven

Although the colon receives little attention from English teachers, good writers make frequent use of the colon. The colon is a dramatic way to gain emphasis for what follows. You should not be reluctant to use it—but only after an independent clause. Unlike the semi-colon, the colon does not require a second independent clause; any lesser word group after it is acceptable. That said, a second independent clause may be used, especially if it is brief.

It's not a good idea to use the colon more than once in a paragraph. In many situations, the dash will work as well as the colon; the colon, though, is more appropriate in formal writing. The reader usually considers the colon a signal that something special will follow.

The colon is used for several minor purposes: for introducing a sub-title, for introducing a long quotation, for punctuating the salutation in a business letter. But using the colon within sentences will make your writing stand out.

Use the Colon to Make Your Point Dramatically

Their response was familiar: no.

The message in a nutshell was this: think.

He made the point again: no more money.

The archbishop stated the challenge: one way or the other, not both.

Although he soon retired, the role General Franks played was particularly important: he was, after all, the commander of CENTCOM.

Use the Colon to Signify the Importance of an Explanation

The professor staggered into the room: drunk.

The weather did not obey the forecast: it rained.

The unemployment rate fell: but not in our city.

Containing identity theft is urgent: it hurts thousands.

In their losing battle, they faced still another setback: their second daughter left home.

It is a comprehensive initiative that will force European leaders to take a stand: join and have some authority, don't join and be ignored.

Use the Colon to Introduce a List

To most Americans, three presidents stand out above all the others: Washington, Lincoln, and Franklin D. Roosevelt.

Three new issues in employment law have arisen: sexual harassment, employee screening, and age discrimination.

To most Americans, the Olympics mean three things: gymnastics, swimming, and track.

In major-league baseball, pitchers now fall into four categories: starters, middle relievers, set-up men, and closers.

America is usually divided into seven regions: New England, the Mid-Atlantic States, the Midwest, the South, the Southwest, the Mountain States, and the West Coast.

The following sentence patterns should be avoided.

To most Americans, the three presidents who stand out above all others *are*: Washington, Lincoln, and Franklin D. Roosevelt.

The regions of the country are very different, *including*: New England, the South, and the West Coast.

Some cities are very cosmopolitan, *such as*: New York, New Orleans, and San Francisco.

Use the Colon to Highlight the Unexpected

The non-denominational chapel had the symbols of the three major religions in the city: the Christian cross, the Jewish Star of David, and the Moslem crescent moon.

There are no guarantees but there are qualities that can work for you: be visible, be pleasant, be productive.

The college caters to several groups: students who work, mothers who are empty nesters, professionals who need further training.

He said it over and over again: you must diet, you must walk, you must talk to one another.

First Draft

Senator Barack Obama's father came from a village in eastern Kenya. It is a village of the kind that can be found throughout rural Africa, with its dirt roads and lack of modern kitchen appliances, such as stoves, refrigerators, and microwaves. It forces a lifestyle that is much harder on the women than on the men.

Possible Revision

Senator Barack Obama's father came from a village in eastern Kenya. Throughout rural Africa there are similar villages: no paved roads, no stoves, no refrigerators, no microwaves. It forces a lifestyle that is much harder on the women than on the men.

Practice

In a daily newspaper, find three sentences in which the colon is used. Write three sentences of your own that have the same structures as those in the newspaper.

A Bump in the Road: Use the Dash

Don't be afraid to use the dash. Your English teacher might not have liked it, but dashes are completely respectable. The dash is a legitimate way to set off interesting but non-essential information. The single dash or a pair of dashes interrupts the flow of a sentence. While the information given may be non-essential, the interruption itself has value, because it changes the voice and tone, giving the sentence a different sound from the sentences before and after.

The pair of dashes in the middle of a sentence is rather dramatic. You're going smoothly along—suddenly a bump—and something unexpected is introduced. That interruption by a pair of dashes is like the voice of a friend breaking in while you speak. Without invitation, the friend adds to—or contradicts—what you've been saying.

The single dash at or near the end of a sentence may be even more dramatic. It might be followed by only a word or two. Those words can add emphasis to what's been said—big time. Or they can undercut the statement that's gone before.

You should use the dash in a way that won't affect the grammatical integrity of the basic sentence. Check this by reading the sentence without the material set off by the dashes; if what is said makes sense, you've got a perfectly good sentence. It's best for the added information to be in a form smaller than an independent clause. If you start to add an independent clause, it probably should be made a separate sentence.

Use a Single Dash at the End of a Sentence for Dramatic Effect

We want it to be there for us—always.

He thought the company had treated him well—until yesterday.

He said he'd always be there for us—like fun.

Although the beheadings were gruesome, we could actually see them—courtesy of the Internet.

The prospect of going to jail simply for doing what a journalist is supposed to do is intimidating to any journalist—indeed to any citizen.

That the court would award workmen's compensation seemed very unlikely—until the plaintiff groaned.

Another possibility was to persuade the plaintiff to retire—and stay retired.

Any misfortune might push a poor family over the edge—an illness, a car breakdown, a flooded basement.

Use a Single Dash to Say More about a Key Word

Those are the *places* where the real work of city government gets done—*places* citizens can't get into, even if they knew where they were.

Phone companies are trying to outdo the cable companies by installing a network of fiber optic *lines* that will reach millions of American homes—*lines* able to carry not only phone calls but also television programming and Internet connections.

New York, New Orleans, and San Francisco are *cities* that are really cosmopolitan—*cities* that are racially, ethnically, economically diverse.

Use a Pair of Dashes for a Brief Elaboration

Sometimes a leak to a journalist has its origins in the most powerful place in the government—the Oval Office—for the purpose of getting revenge against a critic who matters.

Soon the results of a new study will show—right here at home—how rough the past three years have been.

Homeland Security officials emphasize that the fingerprinting and photographing of visitors arriving from Europe is quick—typically no more than fifteen seconds—and easy; the fingerprints are taken digitally, leaving fingers clean.

He felt he had to move on to Plan B—a combination of action and reaction—before making an announcement.

The study will show that 9.2 million working families in

this country—one out of every four—have earnings that are so meager they are barely able to survive.

The recent rebukes of the congressman from Texas—two this week and one last week—have resounded through the House, creating animosity between Republicans and Democrats that is more bitter than usual.

Use a Pair of Dashes to Give Examples

The storm system, which pelted the region with pea-size hail, caused ninety vehicles—cars, trucks, buses—to slam into one another.

Although it might seem obvious, there are a lot of people—lawyers, doctors, professors, coaches, curators—whose career choices add value to our culture.

He says bitter things because he's envious of someone else—the mayor, the governor, our two senators—or because he just can't help himself.

For county residents, the incorrect fee was the latest of a series of mistakes—raises in auto insurance rates, mixups with mail, lost voter registrations—caused by sharing a ZIP code with an adjacent city neighborhood.

Use a Pair of Dashes for a Brief Contrast

A number of couples—but not us—took weekend trips.

The Red Sox—not the Yankees—were favored.

The United States once had many friends—in the days before Iraq—but now it is down to a dozen or so.

Researchers on race now say that what they have found should silence those who believe that in-born inferiority—or superiority—lies behind racial differences in such things as academic achievement, family stability, or criminal behavior.

The mayor had no problem listening to anyone's views—even if they were the opposite of his—so long as they did not get personal.

Outstanding Examples

The president's certitude—that he can see into men's souls—was disturbing; his opponent's certitude—that he will get more done—was equally disturbing.

Some bishops—the shepherds of a church whose hierarchy bungled the molestation and rape of so many young boys by tolerating it, covering it up, enabling it, excusing it, and paying hush money—are doubtful whether those who brought up such matters should receive communion.

First Draft

The movie business has undergone dramatic changes. Some of the causes of the changes are: the coming of the Internet, the invention of the DVD, and the popularity of video games. Another cause is the concentration of theater ownership. You seldom find a stand-alone movie theater anymore. Most movies are shown in multi-screen complexes. While there are more screens than ever before, the complexes are also places with art galleries, amusement arcades, and restaurants.

Possible Revision

The changes in the movie business have been dramatic—a total transformation from what it used to be. New technology has been mainly responsible—the Internet, DVD, and video games. Another factor is the demise of the stand-alone movie theater. The multi-screen complex is now the place to see movies—almost all made by the large studios. And the complexes—usually located in the suburbs—are more than movie venues: they are art galleries, amusement arcades, restaurants.

Practice

In a daily newspaper, find three uses of the dash. Write three sentences of your own that have the same patterns.

Like It—or Not:
Use Like or Unlike

Good writers want to be able to put what's in their minds into the minds of readers. Conveying an idea or an image from one mind to another without the slightest misunderstanding takes considerable skill and experience with language. One technique that is often helpful is comparison and contrast, the pointing out of similarities and differences. That's why in conversation, we're always saying this sort of thing: He looks like the governor, she talks like a lawyer, Paris is not like New York. In conversation, we compare and contrast so often we're not even aware we're doing it. We do it because it helps us to communicate.

A good writer is always on the alert for an opportunity to point out a similarity or difference. Unlike speech, which we can't rewind and revise, writing gives us the opportunity to signal the reader at the beginning of a sentence that a comparison or contrast is coming up. We do this by using the words *like* or *unlike.* If opportunities have been missed in the first draft, look for them as you re-read. A well-stated comparison or contrast helps the reader understand your point and raises the reader's opinion of the writer.

Compare and Contrast the Same Kinds

Like John Travolta, Gene Kelly danced and acted.

Like Oprah, Barbara Walters is an excellent interviewer.

Like Judge Doheney, Judge Silber had little tolerance for misstatements.

Like New York, San Francisco is very diverse.

Unlike John Kennedy, LBJ was not a very good speaker.

Unlike baseball, football is violent on every play.

Unlike an apartment, a house requires constant maintenance.

Unlike representational art, abstract art does not present a familiar image.

These are simple sentences, but experienced readers appreciate them. Each sentence sets two of the same kind side by side. Most often the two things being compared or contrasted will be single-word nouns, but phrases or clauses also can be used as nouns. Such phrases or clauses also should be in parallel grammatical forms.

It is surprising how often thoughts like the ones in the above examples can get tangled up and cause writers to produce illogical statements. That usually happens when the writer wants to give additional information about the first person, place, thing, or idea. There's nothing wrong with that, but the writer has to keep control over the sentence. The writer has to remember that after the additional info is given the second element has to be of the same kind and in the same grammatical form as the first. It is particularly easy to slip up on this in the writing of a first draft. In saying something more about the first thing mentioned, the writer loses track of what it is being compared or contrasted with. This happens to even the most experienced writers.

Writers and editors for *The New York Times* are among journalism's best. Yet defective sentences, like the following, occasionally get past both the writer and the copy editor:

"Like the *transformation* from wagons to rails to aircraft, *we* are changing from wood to oil and now to renewables."

The writer led readers to believe the sentence would present a comparison of transformations, not a comparison of a transformation with *we.* A better sentence would be the following: Like the *transformation* from wagons to rails to aircraft, another *transformation* took us from wood to oil and now to renewables.

Another *Times* writer lost control of this sentence: "Like most of the extraordinary *events* in his life, *he* shares credit for his new venture with . . . ." The writer is comparing events with *he*, a person. That's not a logical comparison.

A *Times* front-page story told about the year-late claim of a $46 million-dollar multi-state lottery prize. The writer wanted to contrast the good luck of the winner with the bad luck of Mr. Patel, the manager of the store that sold the winning ticket, and so wrote this sentence:

"Unlike the *winner*, his *timing* was a bit too far off."

The sentence should have been set up to contrast good timing with bad timing or the winner, a person, with Mr. Patel, another person.

Here's one from the *Times* sports section, about the tennis star Venus Williams:

"Unlike *others* in her position, however, her *growth* spurts and sputters in maturity have been caught on film." The writer set up a contrast between other female athletes and Venus, but the writer never followed through by naming Venus.

Venus must do something to writers. Here's another contrast that hit the net: "Unlike last *year*, when she celebrated with a victory leap, *Williams* was more reserved this time." Contrast a year with a person?

Here's a sentence from a movie review: "Unlike most coming-of-age *stories*, where the male lead serves as a bridge between the confines of a girl's family and the free republic of grown-up love, *Henry* happens to be the long-lost father she has crossed the ocean to meet." What's the point in contrasting *stories* with *Henry*?

What follows are some tough-to-write sentences in which the writer did not lose control.

"Like the *Republicans*, who traditionally have been more allied to the military, the *Democrats* too honored our fighting men."

"Like the *man* who was unaware that he was writing

prose all his life, these *writers* may not know that they are Keynesians—but they are." A writer is logically being compared to writers. The potential for losing control of that sentence was pretty high. But comparing the *man* to *writers* is perfectly logical.

"Unlike most publishing *companies*, which announce their coming titles with great fanfare months in advance, *Barnes & Noble* has kept most of its publishing plans a secret." Most companies are contrasted with one company. Makes sense.

"Unlike their more cosmopolitan *cousins* from Germany, Eastern European *Jews* tended to stick closer to their communities and remain more observant." People are being contrasted with other people, and that's logical.

"Unlike *Alan Keyes*, who beat him in the Maryland Republican senate primary, *Gene Zarwell* had an easy-going style, never paid himself a salary, and never got publicly angry with his own party." That is an excellent sentence, combining an effective contrast and effective parallelism.

An Outstanding Example

"Like *Death of a Salesman*, for example, which exposed the darkness under the sheen of American capitalism, and *The Crucible*, which attacked in symbolic fashion the tyranny of American righteousness, *The Man Who Had All the Luck* is an admonitory work, one that pleads seriously for a national acknowledgment that we are not a chosen people but a fortunate one and declares that our fortune must be wielded with responsibility and without clucking." (Bruce Weber, *The New York Times*, May 2, 2002.)

Now that's good writing. The writer compares two plays with a third one, and in between makes an insightful comment about the second—all in one sentence. That's a writer with control. Nine innings, no walks.

First Draft

A lot of people now pay their bills via the Internet. People have always had bills to pay. Not too long ago the neighborhood merchant was generous with credit, and when you had some money on payday you walked from store to store and paid off your debts. Now a lot of people never see anyone from the company they owe. They don't even mail a check. They pay their bills with a couple of mouse clicks. And along come electronic statements. That means you won't be receiving those fat envelopes from the bank any more. They're going to try to save money by not sending your cancelled checks back to you. Instead you'll have to have a computer and get on the Internet.

Possible Revision

Electronic bill-paying has been around for a few years. Now we're getting electronic checking-account statements. People didn't always pay for things at the time they bought them. It wasn't long ago when neighborhood merchants would keep a "tab" for people who were short of cash but needed to make a purchase. *Like* the grocer, the pharmacist would extend credit, and when people got their pay envelopes they would walk through the neighborhood and pay off what they owed. *Unlike* bill-paying, reconciling a bank statement is a relatively new practice. Before World War II, far fewer families had checking accounts than have them today. *Unlike* bill-paying, which had to be done, reconciling the bank statement did not have to be done. *Like* people who never count their change, some people trust the bank never to make a mistake. For others, the arrival of the fat envelope with cancelled checks was something of an occasion. You could go through the checks and see whom you sent money to during the past month. The cancelled checks were also receipts; you had a piece of paper that proved a payment was made. Now those cancelled checks are no longer being sent out. *Like* the paying of bills, making sure your balance is right will require a computer.

Practice

Make the following sentences more logical, not necessarily sticking to the *like* or *unlike* pattern.

Like the transformation from wagons to rails to aircraft, we are changing from wood to oil and now to renewables.

Like most of the extraordinary events in his life, he shares credit for his new venture.

Unlike the lottery winner, his timing was a bit too far off.

Unlike other star athletes, her growth spurts and sputters in maturity have been caught on film.

Unlike last year, when she celebrated with a victory leap, she was more reserved this time.

Chapter Ten

Short and Sweet; Long and Strong:
Vary Sentence Lengths

You might have had an English teacher who repeatedly said, "Keep your sentences short!" Well, short sentences are good, but so are lengthy ones—when they are well constructed and in the appropriate place. Making all sentences short may be helpful advice for a beginning writer, but it needs to be ignored by anyone who aspires to write with style. Keeping all your sentences short is okay for writers who are capable only of putting together the basic straight-on subject-predicate sentence. But once you are beyond that and can recognize clauses and place commas correctly, the longer sentence has its uses, namely to state ideas that require more words or to give additional information. When experienced readers begin to read a longish sentence, they hold their breath, fearing that the writer may make a misstep and cause confusion. But when that doesn't happen, the reader applauds. For a correctly put-together longer sentence is a thing of beauty.

Brief sentences too can be beautiful. But their beauty won't be appreciated if most of the sentences in a paragraph are also brief. The best uses of brief sentences are as the topic sentence at the beginning of a paragraph, as the concluding sentence at the end, or in the middle between lengthy sentences.

Use Brief Sentences for Emphasis

The shorter the sentence the more emphasis it gets. The longer the sentence, the more what is said is diluted. Don't bury important points in lengthy sentences.

In the paragraph below, notice how the author emphasizes two important points by stating them alone in brief sentences.

As he begins the digital-chip implant procedure, the doctor administers a local anesthetic to a patient and then uses a special injector to place the rice-sized identification capsule under the collarbone or into the triceps. *The injector can also remove the device.* The chip itself contains no patient information, just 256 characters of memory, a radio transmitter, and a tiny antenna. It can be inserted without irritation or infection. A scanner then checks the code and pulls up patient data through the Internet, displaying it on a computer screen. *But privacy is an issue.* The chip is an adaptation of a product used to identify lost pets, track cattle herds, and monitor fish and wildlife, so privacy had not been a concern.

The following paragraph is from "Advice from a Bypass Buddy: A heart surgery veteran offers Bill Clinton *a sneak preview of his new life," by Lance Morrow (*Time*, September 20, 2004). Notice the use of the three brief sentences, especially as they contrast with the three-line-long last sentence.*

"You may find yourself falling into illogical depression and inexplicable rage. We all should be grateful for this gift of time, but for some reason the operation lays one emotionally low. *Watch it.* But most of these things—the weakness, the rage—will pass. You will probably start eating burgers and using salt again, and entertaining the only slightly chastened idea that you are immortal. *You will think yourself bionic. Strength will return.* The adaptable heart will develop what they call collateral circulation (clever new paths of blood flow), and you will find yourself thinking about rafting down a wild river or climbing Everest (don't do it, not enough oxygen), in order to test your wonderful new coronary gizmo."

Use Brief Sentences at the Beginning and End

The brief sentence is particularly effective at the beginning and at the end of a paragraph. Usually, a brief first sentence at the beginning is the topic sentence of the paragraph; a brief final sentence states or implies the conclusion.

The following paragraph is from J. C. Furnas, *Voyage to Windward: The Life of Robert Louis Stevenson.* Notice the difference in lengths between the first and last sentences, on the one hand, and the third sentence, on the other.

"*Vicarious parenthood was also fruitful.* Louis and twelve-year-old Lloyd had got on well at Silverado—under amusingly gypsyish conditions. Life at Davos was more trammeled by weather, walls, and gossipy strangers, bound to arbitrary times, punctuated by crises—Louis's hemorrhages and fits of weakness, Fanny's troubles with her heart, which disliked the altitude, and her growingly surly abdominal tract. Under such strains, not to mention those of a "broken home," the boy persisted in candid hero-worship of Louis as a stimulating big brother. It survived even Louis's attempts to tutor him, though better judgment procured him local consumptive tutors glad to earn while treating their lungs. *Better still, in April he was sent to school at Bournemouth.*"

Notice the mixing of brief and longer sentences in the following paragraphs.

Identity theft has become a major problem. It is a crime that is becoming more and more sophisticated and more difficult to stop. One reason is that clicking on the Internet has become almost as common as turning on the TV. That allows a huge number of people to do their banking and other financial dealings online. Often those transactions involve tapping in bank account and credit card numbers. *Identity thieves live for those moments.* They know a lot more about what can be done online than do Internet amateurs, whose account numbers and PINs, without their knowledge, appear on the thieves' screens. Unfortunately, most of the time the bad guys are able to practice their thievery with impunity. Only sporadically have local and federal law enforcement agencies been able to coordinate their efforts and put identity thieves out of business. *Much more has to be done—and soon.*

Multitasking is stressing us out. Too many people are trying to do too much. We feel compelled to juggle as many commitments as we possibly can, and, as a result, have little time to catch our breath—to relax. What happens when we get locked into years of doing too much? Having many tasks to do means that the body has to deal with constant surges of adrenaline and cortisol, the two major hormones triggered by being in stressful situations. Researchers have deliberately stressed rats to the point of letting them have little time to rest. As a result, they became nervous wrecks, their immune systems weakened, and the nerves in the hypocampus sector of their brains shrunk and ultimately stopped functioning. *Humans suffer similar reactions.* All the cortisol can lead to the production of cytokines, a protein linked to inflammation, depression, and heart disease. *Another result is lowered thyroid activity.* Since the thyroid controls metabolism—the process through which energy is made available—this is a particularly unfortunate result. *We definitely need to slow down. We're burning out.*

Practice

Find a paragraph of your own that you know could be better written. Revise it to vary the lengths of sentences, and also make use of any other techniques discussed in this book that would be appropriate.

Keep Your Eye on the Subject:

Use Subject Repetition to Focus Paragraphs

Paragraphs often fall apart because the writer loses control of what he or she wants to focus on. We tend to free associate as we write, and things slip in that, for the sake of coherence, we should have kept out. We write sentences that go from one thing to another—from one issue to another, from one person to another, from one event to another.

But when you read a paragraph over which you've lost control, the fix is not too hard. Take a look at the subject words of your sentences. If you have a string of different subject words when it was your intention to focus on one thing, your paragraph will lack unity and coherence. One way to revise for unity and coherence is to repeat the name of the thing the paragraph is supposed to be about. Make the subject of the paragraph the subject word of most of your sentences. That will keep the focus on your intended subject.

Don't hesitate to use a pronoun or a substitute noun as

the subject word. When the subject word of most of your sentences is the noun you started with or a pronoun or an equivalent noun, that's what the paragraph will be about, and the paragraph will hold together. When a reader gets confused, it is often because the writer has lost control of his material. When the reader can get through a paragraph without any confusion, the writer has had his material under control.

Study the paragraphs below and note how the repetition helps maintain the focus.

Habeas corpus is a court order requiring proof that a person in custody is being detained legally. For hundreds of years, *habeas corpus* has served as a check against arbitrary and unlawful detention. *Habeas corpus* is one of the few civil rights written into the original text of the Constitution (Article 1, Section 9). In the decades prior to the American Revolution, colonists too often were detained without being charged, and the founders wanted to make sure that practice was ended. But the writers of the Constitution knew that circumstances might arise when there would be no realistic alternative to a suspension. *Habeas corpus* was suspended by President Abraham Lincoln in 1861. Lincoln feared that the Union cause in the Civil War was threatened by Confederate sympathizers in Maryland. *Habeas corpus* would give them the freedom they needed to plot attacks against Washington, D. C.

During the Vietnam War, the two largest cities of what was then North Vietnam were bombed repeatedly by American planes. Haiphong was the important port, receiving supplies from the Soviet Union, and *Hanoi* was the capital, as it still is today in a united Vietnam. But *Hanoi* today is a city of friendship and healing; little hostility toward the enemy remains. *Hanoi* today seems to live by the spirit of forgiveness and healing. The first impression visitors from America get of the city that was the recipient of thousands of American bombs is that the mood is upbeat. The *city* is open for business, hopefully with the former enemy. With conditions improving markedly since the lifting of the U. S. trade embargo, *Hanoi* shows obvious signs of progress. Perhaps the most obvious is the movement away from the formerly ubiquitous bicycle to the newly ubiquitous motorbike. Two decades ago, almost every person and every thing moved by bicycle. Now *Hanoi* has an abundance of cars, trucks, and buses.

An inducement *prize* offers many advantages. *It* attracts attention and considerable effort from contestants. *It* motivates them to spend irrational amounts of time, effort, and cash. *It* needn't cost the organizer much, because he can buy "hole in one" insurance; if the stated goal is reached the insurance company pays the big prize. The inducement *prize* given by the X Prize organizers was obtained through just such insurance. The premium was $1 million but they were able to offer a prize of $10 million.

The country's leading booster of jazz is Wynton *Marsalis*. Now *he* has been honored by being named the artistic director of jazz at New York's Lincoln Center. In that role, *he* will be the caretaker of the new $128 million three-theater complex in the nearby new Time Warner Center. From childhood, *Marsalis* has been under the influence of such venerable heroes of jazz as Dizzy Gillespie, Miles Davis, Art Blakely, and John Lewis. In recent years, though, *he* has been ridiculed for saying that jazz had been diluted by rock, funk, new-age music, electronics, and abstraction. *He* has been called a purist scold who wants to white-out all the innovations that have taken place since the 1960s. With his enrollment at Julliard in 1979, *he* was noticed immediately for his virtuoso trumpet. *He* played with Art Blakely's Jazz Messengers, formed his own quartet, and was signed by Columbia records. Today, *Marsalis* argues that any good jazzman has to be thoroughly familiar with the history of jazz. *He* insists it's necessary to know about New Orleans funeral parades, down-home blues, and, of course, Duke Ellington. *He* believes that contemporary critics and audiences have had a destructive effect on that tradition.

Joe Louis (1914-1981) was known as the Brown Bomber. *He* was a man with a powerful punch, whether a short left jab or a roundhouse right. Born in Alabama and raised in Detroit, *he* left school early and went to work at demanding physical jobs. *Louis* became a professional fighter in 1935, and had twenty-three knockouts in his first twenty-seven fights. In June 1936, *he* took on the German heavyweight Max Schmeling, whom Hitler had embraced as a sterling masculine specimen of the master race. After twelve grueling rounds, *Louis* was knocked out. The loss was a huge disappointment to black people all across the country. But in the rematch a year later, *Louis* knocked out Schmeling in the first round. Once again *he* was the hero of Black America.

"*Athleticism*" is an ugly word. *It* has come to be used more often by sports broadcasters than by writers. *It* is a word that just doesn't make sense to writers, who have time to think about what they are saying. *Athleticism* makes people who have more than just a superficial knowledge of history think about other isms. Fascism, communism, socialism, feminism, racism—all come to mind. *Athleticism* is not like these other isms. *It* refers to ability, specifically athletic ability; the others refer to abstractions, to ideas, often ideas that have had important consequences. *Athleticism*, then, has associations. Writers tend to be more thoughtful about the words they use. Broadcasters who speak of athleticism are usually ex-jocks, who, unknowingly, reveal the poor quality of their educations.

"For Venezuela and its baseball players, *it* is an age of glory, *it* is an age of tragedy, *it* is a period of unseemly riches, *it* is a period of abject poverty, *it* is an era golden with opportunity, *it* is an era black with crime and terror. *Venezuela* is a place where baseball players are worshipped, *it* is a place where players are preyed upon. *It* is a country that, irresistibly calls its players home, and *it* is a country that drives them away." (E. M. Swift, "Unsafe at Home," *Sports Illustrated*, March 7, 2005.)

First Draft

Some employers complain that their workers want nothing less than the perfect job. What is this idea, anyway? What do workers have in mind when they talk about the perfect job? It's a job that pleases the workers on just about all counts. Most people want job security. They don't want a job that will be over in three months, because, for instance, the company merges with another company. Mergers are becoming more and more common in the American economy. Workers say that job protection for the worker is of little concern to the employer. Honesty is another consideration. Workers believe companies hardly ever tell the truth to their employees. They accuse employers of pretending cutbacks are not part of their planning but then they go ahead and lay off people. Also, they say employers promise plenty of overtime but then find ways of getting the work done without paying overtime. Finally, they seem to want to be able to stay home whenever they want to—and get paid. Paying employees for time off surely is part of their perfect job.

Possible Revision

Some employers complain that their workers want nothing less than the perfect *job*. What, then, do they think of as the perfect *job*? *It* is a job that has several basic components. First, *it* is a job they would have for the whole of their working life. The perfect *job* offers perfect job security; which means the worker can never be let go. The perfect *job* not only would pay a good wage but also bonuses three or four times a year, just for doing the job. The perfect *job* also would provide overtime at time-and-a-half whenever the worker wanted it. *It* is a job at which workers want management never to change its mind about anything. Finally, the perfect *job* is a job that pays even when the worker is not on the job. Some employees, their employers say, want to get paid even when they don't come to work.

Practice

Write a 200-word definition of one of the following: bad driving, insomnia, addiction, stress, sexism, careerism.

Or write a 200-word definition of an important concept or write a profile of your favorite celebrity or political figure.

Chapter Twelve

Paragraphs with Style

In each of the five passages below, the writers have used one or more of the techniques illustrated in this book. The use of these techniques clearly raises the level of writing above the humdrum, and gives each passage a certain distinction.

"NYPD Blue" was a detective show loved by detectives. Real cops usually don't watch cop shows; the detectives are unreal, the bad guys too wild, and the sets too clean. But that wasn't "NYPD Blue." Its detectives spoke the language of the station house, it got the bad guys just right, and the language of the station house was the language of real detectives—not a scriptwriter's. Like the detectives on "NYPD Blue," real ones tell a lot of jokes—most of them pretty awful. They razz each other a lot. But when it comes to dealing with outsiders, they pull together. Like those on "NYPD Blue," real detectives spend a lot of time with outsiders: victims, witnesses, suspects. Unlike the scriptwriters' detectives, real ones tread lightly when it comes to getting confessions. They can't threaten, browbeat, or humiliate suspects into confessing. It's against the rules; it can get a detective demoted.

Now that most first marriages usually take place when the couple are in their late twenties or early thirties, one or the other, or both, may have already accumulated substantial assets. Because half of American marriages spin downward into divorce, a prenuptial agreement may be advisable. Just as legalizing a relationship in the first place is a form of protection, so too is a prenup. It's more than a matter of trust; unforeseen events are bound to occur. Relationships change. That's why, once the vows have been spoken, it's a good idea to get to the bank and open three different checking accounts: mine, yours, and ours. Having separate accounts, each spouse can be his or her own person; financial dependency is minimized. Each spouse can spend his or her own money without having to offer a defense. Neither spouse will feel watched. It's not a matter of trust. It's a matter of equality; it's a matter of knowing what individual human beings need emotionally; it's a matter of benefiting from the experiences of others, which would be the height of foolishness to ignore.

Reading the essays of Ralph Waldo Emerson is exhilarating. They are the work of a man who knew life—lots of the bad but also lots of the good. Upon finishing an Emerson essay, countless readers have felt inspired, have felt their confidence boosted, and have vowed for the very first time to be themselves, regardless of what others think. If things were going badly, they could console themselves with the thought that if Emerson could cope with defeat, disappointment, and disillusionment so could they.

The essays reflect the life of a man who had had an unhappy "ugly duckling" childhood. He was aware that his parents, the townspeople, and his teachers thought that his brother would turn out better than he. He was a troubled adolescent: moody, solitary, uncertain. At Harvard, he was a mediocre student, not doing more in his studies than he had to in order to become a tutor, teacher, or minister. Following nine generations of ancestors into the ministry, he disliked doing many of the things expected of a minister— marrying ill-suited couples, visiting sick congregants, burying people whose lives he did not admire. He hated repeating from the pulpit the "truths" of Christianity. To Emerson nothing was settled; everything was up for discussion. Three-and-a-half years after he became pastor of the Second Unitarian Church of Boston, he resigned the position, bade farewell to the ministry, and felt better about himself.

"Over the years, each of B.T.K.'s killings fit a pattern. The killer was diligent, efficient, audacious. He cut telephone lines. He slipped into homes unnoticed—the authorities believe that in at least some of the cases he used fake identification to gain access to his victim's homes. He left his victims bound and killed them slowly.

"Most of all, though, he wrote. For years, B.T.K. sent chilling, taunting letters to anyone, it seemed, who might listen—the police, the local newspaper, the television stations—in which he often left what appeared to be tantalizing clues." (Monica Davey, "After Years of Taunts and Clues," *The New York Times*, February 27, 2005.)

"Thousands of swaths of pleated nylon were unfurled to bob and billow in the breeze. In the winter light, the bright fabric seemed to warm the fields, flickering like a flame against the barren trees. Even at first blush, it was clear that "The Gates" is a work of pure joy, a vast populist spectacle of good will and simple eloquence, the first great public art event of the 21st century. It remains on view for just 16 days. Consider yourself forewarned. Time is fleeting.

"On a partly sunny, chilling morning, with helicopters buzzing overhead and mobs of well-wishers on hand, an army of paid helpers gradually released the panels of colored fabric from atop the 16-foot-tall gates, all 7,500 of them. The shifting light couldn't have been better to show off the effects of the cloth. Sometimes the fabric looked deep orange; at other times it was shiny, like gold leaf, or silvery or almost tan. In the breeze, the skirted gates also appeared to shimmy like dancers in a conga line, the cloth buckling and swaying." (Michael Kimmelman, "In a Saffron Ribbon, a Billowy Gift to the City," *The New York Times*, February 12, 2005.)

About the Author

Paul Marx is Professor Emeritus of English at the University of New Haven, where teaching non-fiction writing was his specialty. His Ph. D. is from New York University, M.F.A. from the Iowa Writers' Workshop, and B.A. from the University of Michigan.

He is the author of *Utopia in America*, and editor of *Modern and Classical Essayists* and *Twelve Short Story Writers*. He has published articles in *The New York Times*, the *Los Angeles Times*, the *Washington Post*, the *Baltimore Sun*, the *Houston Chronicle*, *The New Republic*, *The Nation*, *The New Leader*, *Commonweal*, the *St. Louis Post-Dispatch*, *Dallas Morning News*, *Hartford Courant*, *New Haven Register*, *Yankee*, *Education Week*, *The Chronicle of Higher Education*, and elsewhere.